Teaching Values through PSHE and Citizenship

Activities and Worksheets for Discussions and Debates

John Foster

Brilliant
PUBLICATIONS

Introduction

This book is designed to provide teachers of Years 5–8 with activities that will enable them to fulfil the requirement to promote the spiritual, moral, social and cultural development of children aged 9–13. **Teaching Values through PSHE and Citizenship** presents activities which promote the fundamental values of democracy, the rule of law, individual liberty and mutual respect and tolerance of those with different faiths and beliefs.

The book is divided into three sections.

The first section **Beliefs, Values and Behaviour** focuses on what attitudes and values the children believe should determine behaviour towards others, on the qualities they admire in other people, on what they consider to be good manners and on what they take into consideration when making important decisions.

The second section **Rules and Responsibilities** focuses on the rules that govern people's lives and the responsibilities they have as family members, as neighbours, at school and as citizens. It includes activities that encourage children to discuss what sort of country they want to live in, what they consider the government's priorities should be, why we have laws and attitudes to crime and to the police force.

The third section **Respecting People's Rights** looks at human rights, exploring issues of stereotyping, prejudice, discrimination, sexism and racism. There are also activities on respecting other people's religions and cultures and on global concerns.

Many of the activities involve group discussions and it is important that the children should be made aware of how talking about their ideas and listening to other opinions enable them to clarify their thoughts and to learn what are the fundamental values which underpin society.

It is important, too, to set ground rules for discussion to ensure not only that children respect each other's feelings and viewpoints, but also to ensure that the discussion remains focused and is conducted in an orderly way. It is, therefore, suggested that an introductory lesson is spent discussing the value of talk for learning and drawing up the ground rules for talking in groups.

What Do You Believe?

Aim:
To explore the children's beliefs about how people should behave.

Explain that how you behave depends on how you believe a person should behave, on your ideas about what is good behaviour. Put two columns on the board and ask the children to give examples of what they consider to be good behaviour and bad behaviour and make lists of their ideas.

Give out copies of **Activity Sheet 1 – I Believe**. Ask individuals to go through the list of statements putting a tick beside those that they agree with and a cross against those they disagree with.

Then focus on each statement in turn and ask them to put up their hands to indicate whether they agree with the statement and then discuss the reasons for their views. For example, the reasons why people believe that you should respect other people's opinions include the rights we have to freedom of expression and to think what we like.

Encourage them to add any other strong beliefs that they have to the list. For example, a belief that any form of torture is a crime.

Ask the children:
Which of the beliefs do you hold most strongly?
Invite individuals to say which beliefs they hold most strongly and why.

Encourage them, in groups, to discuss their beliefs, to write them out on slips of paper and to glue them to a large sheet of paper to make a poster of *Our Beliefs*. Then put the posters up in the classroom.

I Believe

Put a tick beside the statements you agree with and a cross against those you disagree with.

That you should respect other people's opinions. ☐

That it is wrong to discriminate against people because of their sex. ☐

That people with disabilities should be treated the same as everybody else. ☐

That you should be able to make fun of people's religious beliefs. ☐

That you should not gamble. ☐

That you should not swear. ☐

That you should always tell the truth. ☐

That you should always put yourself and your family's interests first. ☐

That any form of fighting is wrong and you should refuse to do any military service. ☐

That you should be prepared to stand up against injustice even if it means going to prison. ☐

That cheating is okay if you can get away with it. ☐

That you should not steal other people's possessions. ☐

Teaching Values Through PSHE and Citizenship

What Qualities Do You Value?

Aim:
To explore the personal qualities that the children value.

Explain that people have different qualities. For example, some people are patient, while others are impatient. Some people are quick-tempered, while others are calm. These personal qualities can be divided into positive qualities and negative qualities. Encourage the children in pairs to identify one or two positive qualities that their partner has. Then, list the qualities on the board.

Ask the children to suggest other personal qualities that they look for in a friend and add them to the list on the board. Prompt them, as necessary, to include the following qualities:

carefulness	cheerfulness	consideration	compassion
courtesy	common sense	determination	earnestness
enthusiasm	fairness	generosity	honesty
sense of humour	intelligence	initiative	loyalty
patience	reliability	respectfulness	trustworthiness

Hand out copies of **Activity Sheet 2 – The Qualities I Value** and encourage individuals to draw up a values pyramid, putting the qualities that they value most at the top of the pyramid and those they think are less important at the bottom.

Share their completed pyramids in a class discussion and agree a class pyramid of *The Qualities We Value*.

Extension Activity
As an extension activity you can ask pairs to make a list of what they consider to be negative qualities and then to share their lists in a class discussion. Prompt them as necessary to include qualities such as selfishness, intolerance, dishonesty, meanness, unreliability.

The Qualities I Value

What are the personal qualities that you value most?

Study the list on the board and make a values pyramid by ranking the qualities in order of importance starting with the most important at the top.

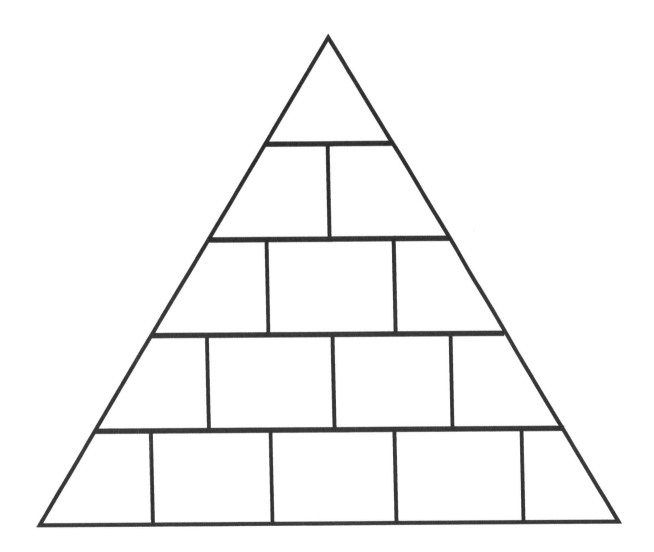

What Attitudes and Values Influence Your Behaviour?

Aim:
To make the children aware of how their attitudes and values influence their behaviour.

Introduce the lesson by asking them to think about how they behave in front of other people.

Are they confident and determined to do what they believe to be right, even at the risk of losing friends and being rejected?
Or are they easy-going and willing to set aside their principles in order to be accepted?

Hand out copies of *Activity Sheet 3 – Attitudes and Values.* Ask individuals to think about each of the statements in turn and to put a tick if they think the statement applies to them, a cross beside the statement if it does not apply to them and a question mark if they are unsure.

Then ask them to write one or two sentences saying what they learned about themselves and their attitudes from the activity.

Encourage children who are willing to do so to share what they have learned about themselves from the activity, but do not pressurise them into sharing if they do not want to do so.

Conclude the lesson by asking which of the statements apply to someone who is strong-minded. Ask the children whether it is more important to stand up for your beliefs and, if necessary, to speak out than not to do something and stay silent, whatever the consequences might be.

Attitudes and Values

Think about each statement in turn. Put a tick beside a statement if it applies to you and a cross beside the statement if it doesn't apply to you. If you are unsure, put a question mark.

I'll do anything to make people like me. .... ☐

I don't care about what people think of me. .... ☐

I'm not prepared to do things just so that people will like me. .... ☐

I want to be accepted for what I am. .... ☐

I won't do things I don't agree with. .... ☐

I want to fit in with the group. .... ☐

I'll go along with anything anyone suggests in order to be accepted. .... ☐

I want to stand up for what I believe in. .... ☐

I'm prepared to say what I think. .... ☐

I'll keep quiet rather than speak out. .... ☐

I'll take the easy way out rather than risk turning people against me. .... ☐

I want to do what is right. .... ☐

I want to make my own decisions rather than to let others decide for me. .... ☐

If everyone else agrees, I'll go along with their decision. .... ☐

I want to be independent. .... ☐

I rely on others to guide me. .... ☐

What Are Good Manners?

Aim:
To explore what is considered to be good behaviour and good manners.

Give out copies of *Activity Sheet 4 – A Question Of Manners* for individuals to complete and then ask the children to compare their answers in a class discussion.

Discuss each question in turn, making the following points:
1. Using a mobile while talking to someone else, such as a shop assistant, is surely bad manners, as is using your mobile while having a meal. Using a mobile in a queue is not bad manners.
2. Eating in the cinema is accepted, though it can be a distraction. Laughing is, of course, acceptable, but talking, especially loudly, is not acceptable.
3. It used to be regarded as bad manners not to give up your seat to a woman if you are a man, and similarly not to give up your seat to an elderly person. Nowadays, people do not always do so. Discuss whether they should.
4. Shouting and swearing is anti-social. Drinking alcohol is banned in some places and whether going round in a gang is acceptable will depend on the gang's behaviour.
5. You should wipe your feet if there's a mat. In some religious buildings you are expected to take off your shoes and in some countries, like Japan it is customary to take off one's shoes before you enter a house.
6. It is good manners to hold a door open for someone who is following you through it, especially if it is a swing door.
7. It is good manners to wait until everyone has been served or you are given permission.
8. You should either wait until after the meal or use a toothpick. You should never use your fingers.
9. It is considered bad manners to put a knife in your mouth in Western society.
10. It used to be considered bad manners to put your elbows on the table, but it is no longer considered to be so.

Extension Activity
As an extension activity, children in groups can draw up a list of advice on mobile phone etiquette – when is it rude to text/speak/play games/surf the Internet on your mobile? When is it acceptable to use your mobile?

A Question of Manners

Activity **4** Sheet

1. **In which of these situations is it bad manners to use a mobile phone?**
    a) when buying something from a shop assistant   **b)** during a meal
    c) standing in a queue

2. **What is unacceptable in a cinema?**
    a) laughing   **b)** talking   **c)** eating

3. **When should you give up your seat on public transport?**
    a) never   **b)** to a pregnant woman   **c)** to an older person

4. **What is unacceptable behaviour in the street?**
    a) shouting and swearing   **b)** eating or drinking   **c)** going around in a gang

5. **When entering someone's house you should:**
    a) wipe your shoes   **b)** always take off your shoes   **c)** only take off your shoes if asked

6. **When you go through a door in front of someone, you should:**
    a) always hold it open   **b)** hold it open if a woman is following you
    c) only hold it open for a person with disability

7. **If you are having a meal you should not start eating:**
    a) before everyone is served   **b)** until grace has been said   **c)** until given permission

8. **If food gets stuck between your teeth you should:**
    a) use your fingers to dislodge it   **b)** wait until after the meal to remove it
    c) use a toothpick to remove it

9. **When is it acceptable to put a knife in your mouth?**
    a) if some food gets stuck on it   **b)** if you cannot get food to stay on your fork
    c) under no circumstances

10. **When is it acceptable to put your elbows on the table?**
    a) at any time during a meal   **b)** between courses   **c)** never

Teacher's **5** Notes

Different Cultures, Different Manners

Aim:
To explore how different cultures have different ideas about what constitute good manners.

Introduce the subject of manners by asking the children to give you examples of what they consider to be good manners, eg saying please and thank you, shaking hands with a person you meet, waiting your turn, and examples of bad manners, eg sticking your tongue out, swearing, queue jumping.

Explain that what are considered good manners vary in different cultures. Ask the children if they can think of some good manners that are bad manners in another culture. For example, Orthodox Jews and strict Muslims will not shake hands with someone of the opposite sex.

Hand out copies of **Activity Sheet 5 – Different Cultures, Different Manners** and ask individuals to decide whether or not they agree with the statements, then to discuss their views in groups before joining in a class discussion.

Points you can raise during the class discussion are:
1. Wearing a hat indoors used to be considered bad manners though there is no cultural reason why.
2. Staring is considered offensive in many parts of the world.
3. In Western societies it is acceptable for women to show their legs, though both sexes may be asked to cover them if entering a religious building. Muslim women must cover their legs.
4. Pointing with your index finger is very insulting in certain countries (eg Indonesia and Thailand).
5. This is a matter of opinion. But in some countries there are laws about how to dispose of chewing gum properly.
6. In some countries (eg India) eating with the left hand is not acceptable, because the left hand is used for cleaning oneself after using the toilet.
7. This was considered to be good manners in the past and is still observed by some people today.
8. This is universally accepted as bad manners.
9. This is regarded as bad manners.
10. It depends. People blow their noses in Western societies, but in some countries this is considered bad manners.

Different Cultures, Different Manners

Activity **5** Sheet

Ideas of what are considered to be good manners vary in different cultures around the world. Study this list of statements about good and bad manners and circle whether you agree or disagree with them.

1. It is bad manners to wear a hat indoors.   Agree   Disagree

2. It is bad manners to stare at someone.   Agree   Disagree

3. It is wrong for a woman to show her legs in public.   Agree   Disagree

4. It is insulting to point at someone with your index finger.   Agree   Disagree

5. It is vulgar to chew gum in the street.   Agree   Disagree

6. It is impolite to eat using your left hand.   Agree   Disagree

7. A gentleman should always stand up when a lady   Agree   Disagree
    enters a room.

8. It is bad manners to interrupt when someone else is   Agree   Disagree
    speaking.

9. It is bad manners to barge in front of someone in a queue.   Agree   Disagree

10. It is bad manners to sniff rather than to blow your nose.   Agree   Disagree

Who Do You Admire?

Aim:
To help the pupils to think about who they admire and what makes a person a hero.

Ask the class to write down the name of at least one person they admire. Then ask them to think about why they admire these people.

Ask:
Is it because they are talented?
Is it because they are brave?
Is it because they are successful?
Is it because they are famous?
Is it because they are unselfish?
Is it because they have made a lot of money?

Encourage them to write a sentence saying why they admire these people. Invite them to tell the rest of the class who they admire and why.

Hand out copies of **Activity Sheet 6 – Who Do You Admire?** Ask individuals to select three groups of people whom they admire, then to share their views in group discussions, followed by a class discussion.

Then ask them to think of one person that they consider to be a hero. It could be someone alive or dead. Encourage them to research the person on the Internet. Put the class in groups and ask each of the group to explain who they chose and why. The group must then choose one of the people to put forward as their greatest hero. The groups take it in turns to argue why the person they have chosen should be recognised as the class's greatest hero, before holding a vote.

Finally, talk about how what we value influences whom we admire.

Who Do You Admire?

On your own pick out three groups of people from this list whom you admire. Then share your views in a group discussion.

Nurses and doctors who help treat people with Ebola.

Anyone who is willing to risk persecution by standing up for their religious beliefs.

Bomb disposal officers who risk their lives clearing minefields.

Business people who have worked hard and become millionaires.

People who dedicate their lives to helping others.

People who have disabilities and who live life to the full.

People who oppose dictators.

Whistle-blowers who expose corruption.

People who make the most of their talents.

Carers who spend their lives looking after people who are disabled or very ill.

Conscientious objectors who refuse to join the armed forces.

Journalists who risk their lives in order to report what is happening in war zones.

A person who shows great courage.

Teaching Values Through PSHE and Citizenship

Who Influences You?

Aim:
To make children aware of the people whose opinions they value most and who has the most influence on the way they behave and make decisions.

Begin by asking the children individually to write down the name of the person who they would ask for advice if they had to make a difficult decision about the right thing to do. Then ask them to write down why they chose that person. Invite them to share their reasons.

Discuss how in difficult situations people turn not only to people whose opinions they value, but to people who care for them and are not likely to give them advice that may be harmful.

Give out copies of **Activity Sheet 7 – Who Influences Your Decisions?** for individuals to complete. Then compare their rankings.

Ask the class:
Who influences you most – your family or other adults?
Your contemporaries or adults?
Which adults influence you most?

Talk about who they would be influenced by:
❑   if they had a problem with a family member
❑   if they had a problem with a friend
❑   if they had a problem at school.

Who Influences Your Decisions?

Who influences you most when you have a difficult decision to make?

Study the list of people who may influence you when you are making a decision. Rank the people who influence you the most, starting with 1 for the person who has the most influence.

☐ Your father

☐ Your teacher

☐ Your mother

☐ Your best friend

☐ Your carer

☐ Your best friend's mother or father

☐ An elder brother or sister

☐ A youth leader

☐ A trusted adult who is a family friend

☐ The head of your local religious community, eg a vicar, a priest, an imam

☐ Another relative (eg an aunt, an uncle, a grandparent)

☐ A local police officer

How Do You Make Decisions?

Aim:
To explore the reasons children give for deciding whether or not to join in with what the rest of a group wants to do and to discuss which are good reasons.

Begin by asking the children to think about situations when they have been members of a group and they have had to make a decision about whether or not to join in with what the rest of the group wants to do.

Talk about tricky situations which may occur because the group wants to do something you don't agree with because it will cause damage or lead to someone being hurt and you may get into trouble.

What influences you most in making a decision about what to do – your own sense of what is right and wrong, what other people in the group will think if you don't join in or your concern that it might get you into trouble.

Give out copies of **Activity Sheet 8 – Making Decisions**. Ask individuals to draw two columns on a sheet of paper, one labelled *Good Reasons* and the other labelled *Poor Reasons*.

Read out the reasons each child on the Activity Sheet gives and ask students to think about them. If they think it is a good reason put the child's name in the *Good Reasons* column. If they think it a poor reason, put the child's name in the *Poor Reasons* column.

Then compare what they think are good and poor reasons in a class discussion.

Ask:
Which of the children gives the best reason?
Which of them gives the worst?

Making Decisions

I join in with what the others want to do because I don't want to let them down.
Kirsty

I go along with what the others suggest. I let them decide for me.
Lucas

I think about what the consequences will be for me if I join in and how it will affect other people.
Alex

I think about whether what's being suggested is right or wrong.
Dinesh

I always try to think what Mum and Dad would advise me to do and what they would think of me if I joined in.
Warren

I think of the risks of getting into trouble. If I think I can get away with it, I'll join in.
Karl

I'm scared that if I don't do what the others want, they'll tease me and call me a chicken, so I go along with what they decide.
Ajinder

I think whether it'll be exciting and fun, or boring and a waste of time.
Corinne

I think of all the reasons for and against doing what has been suggested and decide for myself whether to say yes or no.
Claire

In groups, study the reasons the children give for deciding whether or not to join in with what the rest of their group want to do.
Which of them do you think give good reasons?
Which of them give poor reasons?

What Would You Do?

Aim:
To consider a number of situations in which they would have to make decisions about what to do and how their attitudes and values would influence their decisions.

Hand out **Activity Sheet 9 – What Would You Do?** and ask individuals to complete it.

When they have finished, discuss each situation in turn and ask students to explain what they would do and why.

Talk about the difference between assertive behaviour, in which they would stick to their beliefs and values no matter how others may respond to their actions, and passive behaviour, in which they would stay silent or ignore what is happening and not intervene because they would be concerned about what others might think of them.

Finally, ask them to count up how many a's they have, how many b's and how many c's.

Point out that if they have a majority of a's, they are willing to be assertive and do the right thing, while if they have a majority of b's and c's it suggests they are less willing to be assertive and would behave passively.

What Would You Do?

Study these situations and put a circle round the way you would be most likely to react in each of them. What would you do?

1. **You are out with a group of friends and one of them makes an offensive remark.**
    a) say you find it offensive   **b)** ignore it   **c)** pretend you agree with it

2. **Two of your friends have quarrelled and are about to start fighting.**
    a) try to stop them yourself   **b)** walk away and leave them to it   **c)** encourage them and enjoy watching to see what happens

3. **You have been in a shop and when you get outside you realise that you have been given too much change.**
    a) go back into the shop and return it   **b)** keep the money   **c)** put the money in a charity box

4. **A neighbour politely asks you to turn down your music which you are playing loudly.**
    a) apologise and turn it down   **b)** ignore her   **c)** turn the music up louder

5. **You put coins into a drink machine and it gives you two cans of cola instead of one.**
    a) find someone to tell them that the machine has given you two cans
    b) keep both cans for yourself   **c)** give the extra can to a friend

6. **A friend aged 13 is small for his age. You are at a circus where under 12s are classed as children. Your friend asks for a child's ticket.**
    a) tell the ticket seller your friend's age   **b)** say nothing   **c)** tell your friend he was dishonest

7. **Someone collapses in front of you as they are walking down the street.**
    a) try to help them   **b)** go and find an adult to help   **c)** do nothing because you don't want to get involved

8. **You are with some friends in a supermarket car park and somebody drives off leaving a bag behind them. You look in the bag and it is full of crisps, biscuits and sweets.**
    a) take the bag into the supermarket and hand it in   **b)** share the items with your friends who want to keep them   **c)** let your friends share the items but refuse to have any yourself

9. **You are with some friends and you see some older boys bullying a younger child.**
    a) try to stop them   **b)** ignore what is happening   **c)** join in

10. **Your watch is broken and an elder brother of a friend offers you an expensive new one at a very cheap price.**
    a) turn down the offer   **b)** say you'll think about it   **c)** buy it

Difficult Decisions

Aim:
To present the children with a number of situations in which they are faced with a dilemma about what they should do and for them to discuss what is the right thing to do.

Explain that you are going to ask them individually to think about a number of situations in which they have to decide what they would do. Hand out copies of **Activity Sheet 10 – What Should You Do?** for them to complete. Point out that they will have to decide whether to tell someone about what they saw or to do nothing.

Then in a class discussion invite them to share their views on each situation.

❑ Situations 1–6 describe acts of vandalism
❑ Situations 7 and 8 are examples of bullying
❑ Situation 9 involves cruelty to animals
❑ Situation 10 is anti-social
❑ Situation 11 is stealing
❑ Situation 12 is both illegal and against schools' rules

Ask:
Are any of the actions more serious than others?
Would the right thing to do be to tell an adult about the incidents?
What might stop you from saying anything?

Discuss the view that it is important always to report incidents like the ones that are described, because if we don't do so, then we are letting people get away with something that is wrong.

Then invite the children to write their views on the circumstances in which they think you should remain silent and the circumstances in which you should speak out.

What Should You Do?

Talk about each of these actions and what is the right thing to do in each case.

Imagine you saw someone:	Do Nothing	Report It
1. Spraying graffiti on the wall of a house		
2. Deliberately pulling up flowers from a flowerbed in a park		
3. Carving their name on a seat in the park		
4. Pulling the stuffing out of a seat on a bus		
5. Throwing stones and breaking a window		
6. Letting the air out of a car tyre		
7. Threatening a person smaller and younger than them		
8. Making fun of someone in a wheelchair		
9. Hitting a dog with a stick		
10. Urinating in a bus shelter		
11. Shoplifting from a supermarket		
12. Carrying a knife into school		

People are sometimes afraid to speak out, because they do not want to be accused of telling tales.
In what circumstances do you think it is better to remain silent?
In what circumstances should you speak out?

Write one or two sentences expressing your views.

_____

_____

_____

_____

Attitudes to Animals

Aim:
To discuss attitudes to animals and what rights animals should have.

Introduce the topic by giving individuals *Activity Sheet 11 – Animal Rights* to complete.

Then split the class into groups and ask each group to focus on two of the issues on which they have strong opinions and to list all the reasons why people might agree or disagree with the statements.

Invite them to share their views on the issues in a class discussion, before asking them to draw up a list of the rights they believe animals have.

Encourage the children to use the Internet to find out what laws there are to protect animals from abuse, neglect or exploitation, for example The Animal Welfare Act, and the work of organisations, such as the RSPCA.

Invite them to research pressure groups such as People for the Ethical Treatment of Animals (PETA), the British Union for the Abolition of Vivisection and Pro-Test, which supports the use of live animals in medical research.

Explain that supporters of some organisations, such as the Animal Liberation Front, are prepared to break the law in order to protest about the way scientists experiment on animals.

Conclude the lesson with a discussion of the tactics used by such organisations, such as targeting scientists and their families and setting free animals from laboratories.

Ask:
Can such behaviour be justified?

Animal Rights

Say whether you agree or disagree with these statements.

		Agree	Disagree
1.	All forms of hunting should be banned.		
2.	Only animals from endangered species should be kept in zoos.		
3.	Experiments on live animals are necessary in order to find cures for human diseases.		
4.	The cloning of animals should be prohibited.		
5.	It is wrong to kill animals so that we have meat to eat.		
6.	Animals should not be trained to perform tricks in circuses.		
7.	Keeping hens in battery cages should be banned.		
8.	People should have the right to keep whatever animals they like as pets.		
9.	Using animals to test cosmetics and household products should be illegal.		
10.	Pets should not be dressed up or taught to do tricks.		

What rights do animals have? Make a list of the rights you think animals have.

_____

_____

_____

_____

_____

Why Do We Have Rules?

Aim:
To explore why we have rules.

Introduce the topic by asking the class to think about different types of rules.

Prompt them as necessary to think for example:
- ❑ of rules we have at home
- ❑ at school
- ❑ when we play a game
- ❑ when we are out and about
- ❑ when we are shopping.

Individually or in pairs invite them to list some examples on *Activity Sheet 12 – What Would Happen If We Didn't Have Rules?*

When they have completed their lists, share what they have written and discuss why we have the rules.

Point out that we have rules:
- ❑ to keep ourselves safe
- ❑ to protect ourselves and our property
- ❑ so that we can play games fairly
- ❑ so that we can live together peacefully.

What Would Happen if We Didn't Have Rules?

Write down a rule there is at school.

_____

What would happen if we didn't have that rule?

_____

Write down a rule you have at home.

_____

What would happen if we didn't have that rule?

_____

Write down a rule which keeps you safe.

_____

What would happen if we didn't have that rule?

_____

Write down a rule which protects your property.

_____

What would happen if we didn't have that rule?

_____

Family Rules

Aim:
To discuss rules there are in families, the reasons for the rules and the responsibility that family members have as a result.

Begin by referring back to some of the family rules that were mentioned in the previous lesson.

Pick out different sorts of rules:
- ❏ safety rules such as *'Don't put things on the stairs,'* *'Never take anything electrical into the bathroom'*
- ❏ rules about how you behave as an individual eg *'Don't slam doors'*
- ❏ rules about how you behave towards others eg *'Don't borrow things without asking,'* and *'Don't say hurtful things.'*

Ask the children, in groups, to share their ideas and to list as many different family rules as they can.

Then give out copies of *Activity Sheet 13 – Family Rules: Reasons and Responsibilities* for pairs to fill in.

Family Rules: Reasons and Responsibilities

Fill in this chart listing some of your family's rules, the reasons for them and your responsibilities. The first one has been done for you.

RULE	Don't talk with your mouth full.
Reason:	It's not nice to see chewed up food in someone's mouth.
Reason:	You may spit out some of the food as you are talking.
Responsibility:	I must wait till my mouth is empty before speaking.

RULE	
Reason:	
Reason:	
Responsibility:	

RULE	
Reason:	
Reason:	
Responsibility:	

RULE	
Reason:	
Reason:	
Responsibility:	

RULE	
Reason:	
Reason:	
Responsibility:	

School Rules

Aim:
To explore what rules a school has and the reasons for those rules.

Explain that the focus of the lesson is rules at school and ask the children what rules there are at school, for example:

- ❑ about how you are expected to behave in class
- ❑ in the playground
- ❑ about items you are not allowed to bring to school.

During the discussion help the children to understand that there are:

- ❑ rules concerned with safety, such as not playing games that are too rough and not climbing on roofs to get balls back
- ❑ rules to prevent anti-social behaviour, such as fighting and kicking.

Give out **Activity Sheet 14 – School Rules** and ask the children in groups to suggest possible reasons for each of the rules.

Encourage them to identify which rules they consider to be the most important and which they consider to be the least important and to put the rules in order of importance.

Extension Activity

As a follow up activity, the children could design posters to put up in the classroom to remind them of certain rules and the reasons for the rules.

School Rules

Activity

14

Sheet

In pairs, discuss each rule in turn and suggest reasons for that rule. Which rules do you think are most important? Which rules do you think are least important?

☐ You must not run inside the school buildings or jump down steps.

☐ The following items must not be brought to school: chewing gum, matches, knives, skates, playing cards.

☐ Coats, hats and scarves must not be worn in school.

☐ Jewellery and make-up are not to be worn in school.

☐ You must not climb on the roof or up poles (except on the climbing frame).

☐ Games in the playground which involve lifting, swinging or carrying children are forbidden.

☐ You are not allowed in the swimming pool area unless you are with a teacher.

☐ Children are not allowed to sell things or to swap things at school.

☐ Fighting, spitting and swearing are not allowed.

☐ You are not allowed to leave the school premises without permission.

☐ You must not go on the field when the grass is wet.

Add any other rules which your school has which are not on the list and discuss the reasons for them.

_____

_____

_____

A Classroom Code of Conduct

Aim:
To discuss what rules you should have about how to behave in the classroom and to agree on a classroom code of behaviour.

Explain that the aim of this activity is for the children to think about what sort of place they would like their classroom to be, what kinds of behaviour will prevent it from being that sort of place and to draw up a list of rules that would help to make it into such a place.

Give out copies of *Activity Sheet 15 – The Classroom Code of Behaviour* and invite groups to come up with ideas which you will then discuss together, before reaching an agreement as a class on a set of guidelines for classroom behaviour.

Someone can then put the list of guidelines on the computer and you can print out enough copies for everyone to have one.

You can also put a copy on the noticeboard to remind everyone of the rules you have agreed.

The Classroom Code of Behaviour

Fill in the noticeboard with rules of how to behave in the classroom.

What Is a Good Neighbour?

Aim:
To share ideas on what makes a good neighbour.

Introduce the topic by asking the children to write a sentence saying what a good neighbour is. Then invite them to share their views.

Prompt them as necessary by reading out the statements (below) and adding the ones they agree with to the list.

- ❑ A good neighbour is someone who is friendly, but doesn't interfere with your life.
- ❑ A good neighbour is someone you can rely on to help you if you are ill or have an accident.
- ❑ A good neighbour will help to look after any communal areas, such as stairways and corridors.
- ❑ A good neighbour will let you borrow things.
- ❑ A good neighbour is considerate and won't make too much noise.
- ❑ A good neighbour keeps their pets under control.
- ❑ A good neighbour respects you, your property and your lifestyle.
- ❑ A good neighbour keeps their garden tidy.
- ❑ A good neighbour is someone you can turn to if you're in trouble.

Ask the children to work in pairs and to think of what is good and bad behaviour as a neighbour. Hand out copies of **Activity Sheet 16 – How to Be a Good Neighbour** and invite them to draw up a list of advice – *Top Tips on How to Be a Good Neighbour.*

How to Be a Good Neighbour

Write your top tips of Dos and Don'ts in order to be a good neighbour in the houses below.

Anti-social Behaviour

Aim:
To discuss what is anti-social behaviour and how it should be dealt with.

Hand out *Activity Sheet 17 - Anti-Social Behaviour.*

Encourage pairs to make a list of all the actions which they consider to be anti-social behaviour, then compare their lists.

Discuss how some actions are more anti-social than others eg urinating in a stairwell is more anti-social than breaking branches off a tree.

Draw up a class list of anti-social acts.

Then discuss how you think someone who is found guilty of anti-social behaviour should be dealt with.

Ask the class to discuss the suggestions on the activity sheet.

Encourage the children to discuss the pros and cons of each way of dealing with anti-social behaviour before writing their views on the best way of dealing with it.

Extension Activity
As an extension activity, invite the children to use the Internet to find out what an acceptable behaviour contract contains and to draft what they think an acceptable behaviour contract should contain.

Anti-social Behaviour

What is anti-social behaviour? Make a list of all the actions that you think are examples of anti-social behaviour.

_____

_____

_____

_____

Dealing with anti-social behaviour

How do you think people who are guilty of anti-social behaviour should be treated?
Which of the following actions do you think would be most effective?

❑ Vandals should be made to repair any damage they do

❑ People who constantly cause trouble in a neighbourhood should be banned
from it

❑ People should be made to sign a behaviour contract and be taken into care if
they break it

❑ People should be given two warnings and then sent to a young offender's
institution if they commit a third offence

❑ Parents should be made responsible for young people whose behaviour is anti-
social and should be fined for not controlling their children

❑ Young people whose behaviour is anti-social should have to attend behaviour
management courses and have counselling about their behaviour

❑ Young people who behave anti-socially should have to wear tags and obey
curfews.

**Write your views on what you think is the most effective way of dealing
with anti-social behaviour.**

_____

_____

What Is a Good Citizen?

Aim:
To discuss what makes a person a good citizen and how a good citizen behaves.

Introduce the topic by explaining that we are all citizens of the country in which we are born, but that most countries allow people to apply for citizenship if they have lived in that country for a long time, but were not born there.

Hand out copies of *Activity Sheet 18 – What Makes a Good Citizen?* and invite the children individually to say whether they agree or disagree with the statements or are not sure.

Ask them to list the five things they consider most important in the list, then to share their ideas in a class discussion.

Encourage the class to draw up their own list of what makes a good citizen, adding any other features that they think make a person a good citizen.

Type up the list on a computer and put it on display.

What Makes a Good Citizen?

Say whether you agree, disagree or aren't sure about the statements below.

	Agree	Disagree	?
A good citizen obeys the laws of the land.			
A good citizen tolerates different religions.			
A good citizen respects other people's political views.			
A good citizen takes part in community affairs.			
A good citizen is considerate and doesn't behave in an anti-social way.			
A good citizen votes in local and general elections.			
A good citizen doesn't interfere in other people's lives.			
A good citizen will take a stand against prejudice and racism.			
A good citizen puts his country's interests first.			
A good citizen pays taxes.			
A good citizen is prepared to fight for his country.			
A good citizen cares for the environment.			
A good citizen will help another person who is in trouble.			
A good citizen will belong to a neighbourhood watch scheme.			
A good citizen will report anyone who is committing, or has committed a crime.			
A good citizen will always help the police.			

Compare your class list 'What makes a good citizen' with this list.

The Law of the Land

Aim:
To understand that laws vary from country to country and to discuss what sort of laws they would like the country they live in to have.

Explain that different countries have different laws. When you are living in a country, or visiting a country on holiday, you must abide by the laws of that country.

Ask the children if they know of any laws in other countries which are different to British laws.

Give them some examples:
❏   in Portugal, it is not a crime to possess recreational drugs for your own use
❏   in most American states, smacking is not illegal.

The laws in a country reflect the values of the people who live there.

Give out copies of *Activity Sheet 19 – What Sort of Country Do You Want to Live in?* Encourage the children to identify those things on the list that they would want a country to have.

Then invite them to share their views in a group or class discussion.
Which of the things on the list do people who live in Britain have?

Ask them what effect it would have on their lives if they lived in a country:
❏   where people did not have a vote
❏   in which they were not allowed to criticise the government
❏   where you could not practice your religion
❏   in which you were not allowed to make a public protest
❏   in which you could be imprisoned without trial
❏   In which girls were denied access to education.

What Sort of Country Do You Want to Live in?

Activity
19
Sheet

Study this list and put a tick beside each of the things you would want to have in a country where you lived and a cross against those things you would not want the country to have. Then compare your views.

☐ A country where you have a vote to choose the government.

☐ A country in which possession of drugs is not a crime.

☐ A country where you are allowed to say whatever you like.

☐ A country where assisted dying is legal.

☐ A country where you have the right to own a gun to protect yourself.

☐ A country in which you can get free medical treatment.

☐ A country where there is an independent police force to protect you.

☐ A country which puts its own people first.

☐ A country where all people are treated equally.

☐ A country in which you can live without fear.

☐ A country where the state controls the number of children a family can have.

☐ A country which does not discriminate against people because of their sexual orientation.

☐ A country where it is illegal to preach hatred.

☐ A country which has the death penalty.

☐ A country where people can practice different religions freely.

☐ A country where there is only one political party.

Teaching Values Through PSHE and Citizenship

Different Forms of Government

Aim:
To make children aware of the different forms of government that exist in countries around the world and that the United Kingdom is a democracy.

Explain that until 1215 England was governed by a King or Queen who was all powerful and that the monarch made all the laws. In 1215, King John was forced to sign the Magna Carta, which gave up some of his power to the barons. Today, we still have a monarch, but the government of the country is run by our representatives, the elected members of the House of Commons.

The United Kingdom's form of government is known as a democracy because the members of Parliament are chosen by elections in which all the adults who are British citizens take part.

Many other countries are democracies, but democracy is not the only form of government. In some countries there are still monarchs with absolute power, in others there are dictators.

Hand out copies of *Activity Sheet 20 – Different Forms of Government*. Go through the activity sheet, explaining the different forms of government and then ask the children to research examples of the different types and to complete the sheet.

Examples are:
❑ Democracy – United Kingdom, USA, France, Germany, Japan, South Africa
❑ Absolute Monarchy – Saudi Arabia, Oman, Brunei, Monaco
❑ Military Dictatorship – North Korea, Syria (under President Assad)
❑ One-Party State – China, Russia
❑ A state ruled by religious leaders – Iran

Different Forms of Government

Which type government do each of the following countries have? Write the name of the country in the space provided for examples.

Iran   North Korea   Japan   Saudi Arabia   Syria   Iraq   Russia
USA   China   Monaco   Germany   Sweden   Great Britain
South Africa   Zimbabwe

A government made up of members of political parties chosen by all the adults who are eligible to vote.
Examples: _____

A government by one person who has seized power and makes all the laws himself.
Examples: _____

A government by a king and other members of a royal family.
Examples: _____

A government run by a small group of people who control the armed forces and decide what laws to make.
Examples: _____

A government chosen in an election in which the people could vote only for candidates from one party.
Examples: _____

A government made up of religious leaders who run the country according to the religious beliefs of the majority of its citizens.
Examples: _____

Which of these would be the fairest system of government?

_____

Elections

Aim:
To help the children understand what a democratic election involves.

Explain that you are going to hold an election for class president in order to help them to understand how an election is held in a democracy.

Discuss what the class president's role is:
❑   to chair regular class meetings
❑   to represent the class on the school council
❑   to take turns with other class presidents showing visitors round the school
❑   to supervise the class monitors and to take up issues with the class teacher on behalf of individuals

Split the class into four groups, each of which has to choose a candidate for the role of class president. Explain that each candidate will have a chance to explain why they think they should be elected.

Before they do, give out copies of *Activity Sheet 21 – Electing a Class President.* Ask groups to study the statements of the four candidates and to decide who they would vote for. Then ask the four candidates from the class to prepare and present the reasons why they think people should vote for them.

Prepare ballot papers with the names of the four candidates on them and explain how they must vote by putting a cross in the box against the name of their preferred candidate.

Appoint two members of the class to be in charge of the voting slips and give them a list of class members so that they can make sure everyone in the class votes only once. (They also have a vote.)

Arrange for a ballot box and a voting booth so that voting is in secret. Appoint two members of the class to count the votes and a third member of the class to be the returning officer, who announces the result of the election.

Electing a Class President

In groups, study the statements by these four children who are candidates for the post of class president. Which of them do you think presents the best reasons? Decide who each of you would vote for.

Trevor

I believe I'm the right choice for class president because I'm good at putting forward my point of view and I'd be a good representative on the school council, because I'm a good listener. I'm easy-going and you could count on me to make the right decisions. I wouldn't let you down. It would be an honour if you elected me as president.

I'm very stubborn so I'd make a good class president. I'd stick up for what you told me you wanted done. I wouldn't be afraid if other people didn't agree with me. I'd be reliable and would always turn up for meetings. Give me a chance. Vote for me.

Naseem

Naomi

I'd be a good class president, because I'm captain of the netball team and I know what it's like to be the leader of a team. I'd make sure that the girls in the class had a say in the decisions and weren't pushed around by the boys. You should vote for me.

My dad's a school governor and my brother's in the infants, so I'd know what's going on in the school. I'd be in a good position to represent you. I'm quite good at speaking and I think I'd be a good president.

Jordan

What Should Government Priorities Be?

Aim:
To explore what their priorities would be if they were in charge of the government's finances and had to decide how to spend a windfall.

Explain the aim of the lesson, then hand out *Activity Sheet 22 – What's Your Priority?*

Go through the statements and invite pairs to take on the roles of MPs with different points of view.

Encourage them to prepare a short speech arguing why they think their cause is the one that the money should be spent on. Then draw lots for the order in which they are to speak. After they have all given their speeches allow anyone who wants to add further comments to do so.

Before you take a vote to decide how the class would spend the money, invite them in groups to discuss what the priorities should be and to choose two of the causes that they think are the most deserving.

Make a ballot paper listing the various causes that the groups suggest and then hold a secret ballot to decide which cause the class chooses to spend the money on.

What's Your Priority?

Imagine that a billionaire tycoon has left his fortune to the state on condition that it is all to be spent on one particular priority area. Discuss the views (below) on how the money should be spent and decide which area you think the money should be spent on.

It should be spent on the arts. A society that values creativity and works of art – paintings, literature, music – is a healthy, vibrant society. We neglect the arts at our peril.

Unless we take action to protect the environment, we will find we have destroyed the Earth through pollution and climate change. The money should be spent on protecting the environment.

We need to build up our armed forces in order to protect ourselves from the threat of ISIS and other extremists. The money should go towards building a new aircraft carrier, fighter jets and increasing the size of the army.

If we really care about the future, the money should be spent on our schools to make class sizes smaller, to improve facilities and give everyone a first-class education.

I'd spend it on developing sport for all. Sporting activities keep people fit and healthy and so the money would be well spent, as it would mean less would be needed for the National Health Service.

The money should be spent on scientific research into diseases such as cancer, Parkinson's disease and into what causes dementia. This would save lives and reduce suffering.

People are living longer and many of them need help. I think the money should go towards the care of older people.

The money should be spent on the National Health Service to provide more doctors and nurses and in hospitals to ensure that everyone gets the best possible health care.

We should give it to people in the poorest nations of the world in international aid. They need it more than we do.

It should be spent on providing more resources for the police in order to combat crime.

What Would You Do if You Were Prime Minister?

Aim:
To get the children to think about issues that concern them and which laws they would like to introduce.

Explain to the children that this exercise is designed to make them think about their values and priorities by asking them what laws they would introduce if they were the Prime Minister.

Prompt them to start thinking about what laws they might introduce to make travelling safer. For example:
- ❑ by reducing speed limits
- ❑ by raising the age at which you can get a driving licence
- ❑ by increasing the punishment for texting while driving
- ❑ by making it against the law to ride a bicycle without wearing a helmet.

Hand out copies of *Activity Sheet 23 – If I Were Prime Minister* for the children to complete.

If I Were Prime Minister

Write down three laws you would introduce if you were the Prime Minister. Explain the reason why you would make these laws.

LAW:

REASON:

LAW:

REASON:

LAW:

REASON:

Civil Law and Criminal Law

Aim:
To make the children aware of the difference between civil law and criminal law.

Introduce the topic by explaining that there are two types of law – civil law and criminal law - and that there are two different sets of courts to deal with civil cases and criminal cases.

Civil law is concerned with private rights and deals with disputes between individuals, for example, over contracts, property and family matters. Criminal law deals with crimes and punishments for criminal offences.

Hand out copies of **Activity Sheet 24 – Civil Cases or Criminal Cases?** Invite pairs to discuss each of the scenarios and to decide whether it is a civil or a criminal matter.

1. This is a dispute over property and, therefore, might be considered to be a civil matter. However. If you cannot get your bike back, your friend could be accused of stealing it, which is a criminal matter.
2. This is a civil dispute. However, it depends what the lie is and if the person will not stop spreading it they may be guilty of a criminal offence.
3. This is a criminal offence.
4. This is a civil matter. The owner of the greenhouse can sue you if you won't pay for its repair, but you are the owner of the ball and are entitled to get it back.
5. This is a civil dispute.
6. This is a criminal offence.
7. This is a civil dispute.
8. This is a criminal offence, provided it can be proved that the person deliberately tried to hurt you.
9. This is a civil dispute about a contract. The company can take you to court if you do not continue with your payments.
10. This is a civil dispute.

Civil Cases or Criminal Cases?

Activity
24
Sheet

In pairs, discuss each scenario and decide whether it is a civil matter or a criminal matter.

Then compare your answers in a group discussion.

	Civil	Criminal

1. You lend your friend a bicycle, but when you ask for it back he refuses to give it to you

2. Someone posts a lie about you on a social media site.

3. Your computer was stolen while you were on holiday.

4. You kicked a ball over a fence and smashed some panes of glass in a greenhouse. The owner of the greenhouse refuses to give your ball back until you have paid for the glass to be replaced.

5. You swapped a computer game with someone for another computer game, but when you tried to use it the one you were given wouldn't work.

6. Someone (you don't know who) vandalised your bicycle.

7. You agreed to sell someone some CDs and gave the CDs to them but when you asked for your money they refused to pay you.

8. Someone tripped you up deliberately and you broke your wrist.

9. You take out a mobile phone contract for a year and after six months you want to cancel it, but the company says you can't and must keep on paying until the year is up.

10. A neighbour complains about you taking a short cut over their property and says they are taking you to court to stop you doing so.

What Do You Think of the Police?

Aim:
To explain why we have a police force and to explore attitudes towards the police.

Introduce the topic by asking why we have a police force.

Prompt the children as necessary and explain that societies have a police force:
- ❑ to ensure that people obey the law
- ❑ to keep order
- ❑ to protect the public and their property
- ❑ to prevent, detect and investigate crime.

Point out that the police will also help people in a crisis or when they are distressed.

Explain that in a democracy such as the United Kingdom the police force is independent and free of state control, whereas in a dictatorship the police force is used by the dictator to suppress opposition and keep him in power.

Invite children to complete *Activity Sheet 25 – What Do You Think of The Police?*

Then compare their answers in class discussion.

What Do You Think of the Police?

Activity **25** Sheet

Do you think the police are helpful and friendly?   **Yes No**

Reason: _____

Do you think the police treat everyone fairly whatever their skin colour?   **Yes No**

Reason: _____

Do you think the police listen to young people? **Yes No**

Reason: _____

Are police officers someone you would turn to in an emergency? **Yes No**

Reason: _____

Do you think the police do a good job? **Yes   No**

Reason: _____

Would you ever consider training to be a police officer or special constable?
Give reasons for your answer.

_____

_____

_____

How Should We Treat Offenders?

Aim:
To explore attitudes towards people who break the law, to discuss what the purpose of punishment should be and what punishments should be given for particular crimes.

Introduce the topic by reminding the children of the difference between civil law and criminal law and that people who break the law are dealt with in criminal courts which can give offenders a variety of punishments. Ask the children to suggest what punishments the courts can give and make a list on the board.

Then ask the class what they think the purpose of punishments should be.
Should it be to make the offender suffer eg by fining or imprisoning him?
To protect society from the offender by making it impossible for him to commit further offences?
To deter the offender from doing it again?
To change the offender's behaviour so they won't offend again?
To repay or compensate the victim?

Hand out copies of **Activity Sheet 26 – Which Punishment?** Before asking individuals to complete it, explain that the list includes flogging and mutilation because in some societies in which there is Sharia law, the punishment for some crimes may be a public flogging and for theft, mutilation (cutting off a hand).

Compare their answers in a class discussion, inviting the children to explain the reasons why they chose the punishments they did.

Ask:
Would it make a difference if the offender was under 17?
It was the person's first offence?
The person was a drug addict or an alcoholic?

Finally, hold a discussion of these two views: a) the victim of a crime should be able to decide what punishment to give the offender; b) the offender and his family should be made to pay the victim's family an appropriate sum in compensation.

New Laws

Here are some suggestions for changes to the laws about children. In groups discuss why you are for or against each proposed change. Then share your views in a class discussion and vote on each proposal by a show of hands to say whether the class is for or against the proposal.

	Agree	Disagree

1. There should be no restrictions on the number of hours children are allowed to work.

2. Children should be able to get a tattoo at any age.

3. Children should be entitled to pocket money by law.

4. No one should be allowed to be a babysitter until they are 16.

5. Children should be allowed to make their own medical decisions.

6. Children who commit crimes should have their sentences decided by the victims of their crimes.

7. You should be able to drive a car at 16.

8. All children aged 16 - 20 should have to spend a year doing national service.

9. You should be able to leave school at 14.

10. You should be able to leave home when you are 12.

Stereotypes and Stereotyping

Aim:
To help the children to understand what
stereotyping is.

Explain what stereotyping is – thinking that all people who come from the same
racial background, the same part of the world or have the same appearance have
similar interests and personalities and all behave in the same way.

Hand out copies of *Activity Sheet 29 – Stereotypes and Stereotyping* for the children
to complete individually, then hold a class discussion in which you take each
statement in turn and discuss how it is an example of stereotyping.

Encourage the class to think of other examples of stereotyping. For example:
❑   all women like the colour pink
❑   all boys who spend hours on the computer are geeks.

Point out that stereotyping can be damaging because it is often based on
prejudice and can lead to discrimination.

Stereotypes and Stereotyping

On your own decide whether you agree or disagree with the following statements. Then in groups discuss which of the statements are based on stereotypes.

	Agree	Disagree

1. People with disabilities are unable to lead fulfilling lives.

2. Red-headed people have quick tempers.

3. Left-handed people are more creative than right-handed people.

4. People who refuse to join the army in wartime are cowards.

5. Everyone from the Caribbean likes cricket and reggae.

6. People who have strong accents are uneducated.

7. Everyone who goes to a public school is a snob.

8. Most criminals come from broken homes.

9. People from India and Pakistan are no good at football.

10. All Scottish people belong to a clan and wear a kilt.

Write a short statement saying what you learned from this activity about stereotyping and saying whether or not you think stereotyping is dangerous. Give reasons for your view.

_____

_____

_____

Judging by Appearances

Aim:
To understand what prejudice is and to discuss examples of prejudice.

Explain that the lesson is about prejudice.

Put the word 'prejudice' on the board and ask the children what it means. Explain that it involves making a judgement before knowing all the facts.

Ask the children how can you tell what a person is like? Hand out **Activity Sheet 30 – Judging People** and ask individuals to complete it.

Then take each feature in turn and ask anyone who ticked that feature to explain why. Explain that the only two features that give a clue as to what a person is really like are the way they behave towards others and what their manners are like. The other features do not reveal their personality and judging a person on them is likely to be because of prejudice.

Ask the class how they judge what a person is like.
What qualities matter more than whether they have tattoos, how they dress and what colour their skin is?

Put the children in groups and ask them to write down their suggestions as to how we can tell what a person is really like:
Are they kind-hearted?
Will they help you if you are in trouble?
Are they honest and trustworthy?
Do they respect your opinion?

Encourage them to make a collage showing examples of prejudice or to write a poem about prejudice. They could write a list poem Prejudice is... or an acrostic, in which the first letters of the lines spell the word 'prejudice'.

Discrimination

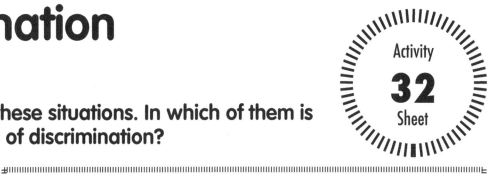

In groups, discuss these situations. In which of them is the person a victim of discrimination?

1. Ian applied to become a pilot but was rejected because he is colour-blind.

2. Chloe applied for a job at an all-night cafe. She had more experience than the man who was given the job, but was not offered the job as the manager wanted a man who would be able to deal with troublesome customers.

3. Trevor and his friend Jason both own identical sports cars. Trevor is Afro-Caribbean and Jason is white. Trevor has been stopped several times by the police though he is careful not to exceed the speed limit. Jason has been stopped only once.

4. Fiona works as a supervisor in a factory. She finds out that she is being paid less than Thomas who does the same job in another of the firm's factories.

5. A businessman is not allowed to enter a restaurant, which has a strict dress code, because he is not wearing a tie.

6. A person in a wheelchair goes into a shop and is unable to get to the department she wants to go to because it is on the first floor which can only be reached by stairs.

7. In a class, the boys are made to sit at the front and the girls at the back.

8. There is a rule that no jewellery is to be worn in school. This includes the wearing of necklaces with a cross on.

9. A person who is distributing anti-gay leaflets outside a school is told that he must stop doing so.

10. A black teenager who is carrying a sports bag containing his sports clothes is stopped by a police officer and asked to open it.

Disability Rights

Aim:
To raise awareness of the rights of people with disabilities and to investigate how they may be discriminated against.

Introduce the topic by discussing what we mean by people with disabilities – people with physical, mental, intellectual or sensory impairments.

Discuss how the disability may be the result of an accident or illness and how some people are born with a disability. Emphasise that people with disabilities should not be defined by the disability and that we should refer to them as people with disabilities rather than disabled people and we should avoid derogatory terms such as 'crippled', 'mentally retarded' and 'wheel-chair bound'.

Hand out copies of **Activity Sheet 33 – The Rights of People With Disabilities** and encourage groups to discuss the rights and to decide which they consider to be the most important.

Ask the class if they know anyone who has a disability. Invite them to share how it affects the person's life and to say whether they think the person's rights are denied in any way. Be aware that some members of the class may prefer not to talk about a relative or friend who has a disability and do not pressurise them to do so.

Talk about how well your school is equipped to meet the needs of people with disabilities.
Are there disabled toilets?
Are there ramps so that wheelchair users do not have to go up steps?
Is there easy access to all the classrooms?

Discuss the provision that is made for people with disabilities on public transport and in access to public places in your neighbourhood.
Are there any places where access is difficult for people with disabilities?
Is there, for example, easy access to the local cinema, to the library and to local shops, cafés and restaurants?

Groups can work together to survey the neighbourhood and to present a report of their findings to the rest of the class.

Which Pressure Group?

You are a committee whose job it is to decide how to split a legacy of £7,500 between 5 pressure groups from a list of 22.

You must decide which pressure groups are to receive the following amounts:

£2500 _____

£2500 _____

£1500 _____

£1000 _____

£500 _____

Compassion in World Farming	Amnesty International	Migration Watch
Oxfam	Electoral Reform Society	Liberty
Society for Protection of Unborn Children		Action on Smoking and Health
Campaign Against the Arms Trade		Christian Aid
Greenpeace	Disability Rights	Friends of the Earth
Shelter	Campaign for the Preservation of Rural England	Fair Trade
British Union for the Abolition of Vivisection		Pedestrian Association
Campaign for Dignity in Dying	Waste Watch	Age UK	League Against Cruel Sports

Lightning Source UK Ltd.
Milton Keynes UK
UKOW07f1806120616

276085UK00003B/54/P